Cancer...It Won't Get The Breast of Me

A Humorous Look at One Woman's Battle With Breast Cancer

Written by
L.S. Coffman

L.S. Coffman

Rascal Treehouse Publishing
Copyright © 2006 by L.S. Coffman
ISBN 0-9759321-4-4

Visit author's website: **www.lscoffman.com**

Printed in the United States of America

This book is lovingly dedicated to all of the Doctors, Surgeons, Nurses, Technicians and Health Care Personnel who so kindly and patiently treated me.

L.S. Coffman

Preface

Before you turn another page it is important that you are made aware of two important factors about this book. First, this book is not intended to be an instructional or informational manual concerning anyone else's treatment for cancer. It is a chronicle of my personal battle against breast cancer and, in no way, should be taken as anything beyond that. Secondly, God has blessed me with an ability to find humor in life's situations and my treatment for cancer was no exception. While I may have embellished certain events for humor's sake, it is not my intention to trivialize anyone's battle with this disease. My treatment was very traumatic and life changing as anyone's would be. But, I know that a positive outlook and humor have gotten me this far and I am winning the battle. There is a lot of power in being able to laugh at things related to your illness in the context of a joke. It gives you the feeling that "I can lick this thing; I may have cancer, but I'm not a victim.

My sole purpose for writing this book is, hopefully, to bring a little laughter to those of you engaged in your own private war with cancer. Throughout my treatment I strived to absorb details of the many tests, scans, biopsies, procedures, etc. I was actively looking for something that could be formed into humor. And I was not disappointed. I know that through most of your treatment you may have no desire to read or even to talk about what you're going through. That was my experience. But, when you get through the darkest hours and the light of day begins to shine again, I hope what I have written will resonate with you and put a smile on your face. And, don't feel guilty if you laugh right out loud.

Chapter 1

A Date With The Booby Trap

The morning I found the tumor in my breast I was sitting on my veranda enjoying Smoked Salmon Eggs Benedict, Ham and Cheese Frittata and Sausage Quiche prepared by my cook and housekeeper, Hazel. All right, all right, I was sitting in front of the T.V. watching Regis and Kelly wolfing down a bowl of Froot Loops! I'm an "average Jane" living in America. At least, more Americans can relate to my life. In telling my story it is important to me that I seem real to you, the reader. I am an avid reader of mystery, thriller, and crime novels and I am sick of every main female character being thin and beautiful wearing designer clothes and her love/hate leading man is always handsome and successful. These characters also eat food that the average American cannot pronounce, much less eat. When was the last time you read where the heroine came home from work and made herself a bologna sandwich and chocolate milk for dinner? They are more likely eating cheese, homemade bread and drinking a fine wine.

But, I digress, back to my bowl of Froot Loops. Many people would call it good luck, or fate but no one will ever convince me that what happened next was anything short of God's intervention. I have never been one to do self-breast exams since I am a well-endowed, buxom woman. I always figured that I had no idea what I was looking for and even if I did I wouldn't be able to find it. I have relied on yearly Mammograms and regular breast exams performed my favorite "groinocologist," Dr. B. She had performed just such an exam about three months prior to this discovery.

Well, as any "fluffy" woman will tell you, it is not uncommon for a sample of everything you eat to end up on your chest. This particular morning that sample was a gift from God. A single drop of milk fell onto my T-shirt over my right breast. When I think back on this moment, I always see it in slow motion. I think that's because I realize, now, how that single drop of milk would change my life, forever. Since falling "debris" has ruined many of my t-shirts and tops, I now try to wipe away the stain, immediately. However, this morning, I felt something I could not remove underneath that spot. You know how I said that I wouldn't know what I was looking for even if I found it? I knew. I knew. It was about the size of those large marbles I used to play with as a kid, distinctively solid and going nowhere. I couldn't admit, at first, that I was feeling this...thing. I kept rubbing it, pressing it until I made it sore. After an hour I knew I had to call my doctor and get in. It had not been there when she examined me. It was located high on the breast and barely under the surface. No one could miss it.

The next morning found me in Dr. B.'s office for another exam. There are some situations where you remember details. I remember the doctor's exact words to me. "This has to be addressed immediately." She asked her staff to call the breast care center and get an appointment for me that same day. They would be performing both a Mammogram and Ultrasound.

Preparing for Your Mammogram
Exercise #1

- Open your refrigerator door and insert one breast between the door and the main box.
- Have one of your strongest friends (or a stranger) slam the door shut as hard as possible and lean on the door for good measure.
- Hold that position for five seconds.
- Don't breathe.
- Repeat again in case the first time wasn't effective enough.
- Repeat all steps on the other breast.

Exercise #2

- Visit your garage at 3:00 a.m. when the temperature of the concrete floor is just perfect (anywhere below 32 degrees).
- Take off all your warm clothes and lay on the floor with one breast wedged tightly under the rear tire of the car.
- Ask a friend to slowly back the car up until the breast is sufficiently flattened and chilled.
- Turn over and repeat for the other breast.

Congratulations! Now you are properly prepared for your mammogram.

Chapter 2

You Are Now Entering Hooterville

The Hooterville Breast Care Center was located...okay; it doesn't matter where it's located. The important thing to remember is that the names have been changed to protect the innocent and the guilty. She said she wanted to be called Ginger in my book. I made a note of that. I wasn't sure if we would still be speaking after she was done with me. And, because the body parts to be examined are personal, I named my right breast, Laverne, and my left breast, Shirley. Laverne was under the gun today. I have to give kudos to Hooterville for supplying me with an extra large gown even though I told her that, at my age, all I needed to do was pull up my skirt! Then Ginger led me into the room with the Booby Trap. It's the only contraption I know of that takes cups and turns them into saucers without having to sweep up glass. Ginger is tall, pretty....oh, who cares? This is about me.

You larger than tiny gals know the drill. I stepped up to the Booby Trap and introduced myself. He didn't care and we all know it's a "he" because a woman would have used this technique to check for testicular cancer. Ginger pulled out the largest shelf she had and invited Laverne to have a seat. Laverne obliged having had the memory of her last Mammo squeezed out of her. As Ginger pressed the button on the floor, I knew what was coming even if Laverne didn't. I was grinding my teeth as the top shelf began depressing Laverne into enough square footage to carpet my veranda! She began to spill over the sides and reminded me of that old fifties movie, "The Blob." Satisfied that she could squeeze no more, Ginger told me to hold my breath and don't move. Now, I must note here that it was not possible to take a breath because my right lung was oozing out my nipple! And as for moving...well that's too asinine to even address. *"I'm ready for my close-up, Mr. DeMille."* Several pictures were taken in different poses and then Laverne was released to wait with me while Ginger put them up for auction on eBay. As we're waiting, I looked down at Laverne and she was as red as a tomato. It took all my self-control to keep from hollering down the hall, "I need a bucket of ice...I'm on fire in here!" Ginger must have found some takers because she returned to take me to the ultrasound room.

Still beet-red and throbbing like a toothache, Laverne had to be dragged kicking and screaming onto the ultrasound table. I tried to assure her there was nothing to be afraid of and promised to take her home, soon. It was in this room that I was informed of another questionable "area of density" on Laverne's underside. This examination concluded after about twenty minutes and I was given an appointment for a biopsy of the two questionable areas for the following Thursday. It was Wednesday of the previous week.

Now, some of you might think I went home and had a crying jag but you would be wrong. I don't remember now but I probably consumed some kind of comfort food. That's how I handle my problems. Eat enough chocolate or ice cream and anything that doesn't look better can usually be diluted with liquor! If this were a typical book, I would now write about my glamorous apartment. I would write about donning silk pajamas, making a cappuccino and curling up on my overstuffed sofa with my Angora cat and the latest N.Y. Times bestseller. But, this is not any story. It's mine and in my life I came home to my little two-bedroom, vinyl-sided house to greet my DoxiePoo, Maxwell. He is said to be the love child of a poodle and a dachshund but he looks more like a black Lab whose legs have been cut off. My first words of greeting are the usual, "Not now, Max, I gotta pee!" If you're over forty-five and menopausal you know what I'm saying. Once relieved, I donned my too-big jersey sleep pants (which will end up on the floor upon the onset of my first hot-flash, or rather, power-surge), and my paint-spattered t-shirt. Not even Maxwell will sleep with me so who cares?

I normally would curl up on the sofa with a mediocre book but this had proved to be a not so normal day. I found that I could not focus enough to read so I turned to television for a mindless diversion. Two hours, two Tylenol PMs and 100 mg. of Zoloft later, I finally succumbed to sleep. Wouldn't you?

The next week seemed blurred to me. I had wanted to keep a journal along the way because I knew I would want to write some kind of book about the experience but my efforts were hit and miss, more miss than hit. From that first day I found the lump I lost my desire to read or to write. These had always been an escape for me from my mundane life. Now, when I needed one, I came up empty. Instead, my days were filled with the screams and laughter of little children because for over twenty-nine years I have run a child day care in my home. It's hard to concentrate on your problems in the midst of all that commotion. I've never been predisposed to worry but I was anxious to get through the upcoming biopsies and get on with my glamorous life. After all, there were noses to wipe and bottoms to clean and nobody does that better than me. I love my work and love my kids. Most of them come to me as infants and continue until kindergarten and for summers after that. I'm being honest with you when I tell you I was as concerned about how the results would affect "my kids" as much as for myself.

Chapter 3

B Stands for Biopsy

It's Thursday, April 28, 2005....B-Day (Biopsy Day). I sat in the waiting area at Hooterville Breast Care Center, alone. I went there alone because I saw no need to take up someone else's time to wait for me. A brief sidebar here, don't try to be as brave as I did. All my life I struggled to keep my emotions in check, never to let anyone see fear, pain or heartbreak. Even when my mother or father would spank me, I would refuse to cry until I absolutely had to. Later, while raising my two sons alone, I found myself, of necessity, hiding my feelings from them to protect their childhood innocence. I would not let their childhood be tarnished with the financial struggles, with the absence of caring grandparents, with my own loneliness and frustrations at their father's absence. It's a lifetime of conditioning that makes it difficult to express emotion in even a situation such as this, for I still had not shed a single tear for myself.

But, I can write what I felt and what I felt that day was fear. I was fearful of the unknown; unknown pain, unknown results and my unknown reaction to those results. I was wishing that I had not come alone. Nobody has to be that brave. If I made light of what I was going through, I thought, those who love me wouldn't be so worried but I think it was a bit of denial for my sake, too.

The clinic was running behind on that particular morning. My appointment was for 9:30 and, being the kind of personality that I sometimes am, I had been there since 9:00 a.m. At 9:30 a staff member poked her head through the door and informed me that it would be a while longer.

"I understand", I replied, while the little voice in my head is barking, "Well, of course you're running late! It wouldn't be a doctor's office without a total failure to run on schedule! I'll keep sitting here on this bed of nails while my imagination continues painting its own interpretation of what you people are going to do to Laverne back there!"

"That's fine, no rush," I said.

At 10:15 the Biopsy Tech came rushing through the door to say she could take me now. After telling her that this experience will be part of a book, I asked her what she wanted to be called in the story. She chose a name I suggested because of her coloring, Nutmeg. Another waist-up strip tease, another huge gown opening in the front, and Nutmeg led me into the sci-fi world of Stereotactic Breast Biopsy. It was a nicely appointed room, countertops around the perimeter, neat and tidy, even an upholstered love seat in muted spring colors. Nothing, however, could draw my focus away from the solitary object that adorned the center of the room. At first glance, it was unassuming, a padded rectangular table covered in faux vinyl with a large hole cut out of the center of one end. By now, I had been talked through this procedure more than once by the staff. I had an idea how this table worked as well as the apparatus that stood sentry under the table opening waiting to be called into action. I also knew that dear Laverne was to occupy that hole.

With all the grace and agility that you would expect from a majestic, full-bodied fiftyish woman, I eased myself onto the table as the petite Nutmeg tried to steady my ascent with both her bony little hands. I looked over my shoulder where her tiny frame was barely visible and warned her that she is overestimating her abilities if she thinks she can break my fall! As this truth was realized, she removed her hands and stepped back out of the target's range. Once on the table, I knew that I was expected to lie on my stomach with Laverne dangling through the hole in the table. Now, Laverne can hold her own in the size department so this was much like threading a needle with mittens on! Stop reading here and get a mental picture.

Got it? Okay.

"If this is One-Size-Fits-All you are in for a shock," I called over my shoulder.

"Get comfortable," instructed Nutmeg.

Yeah, right. My greatest concern at that point was there could be a video camera somewhere in that room that was recording my acrobatics to entertain at the company Christmas party!

Once in position, two shelves were mechanically moved toward each other with, guess who, in between. Yep. You got it. Laverne was about to become a prisoner dangling through that hole! This was reminiscent of the Booby Trap but on a much more bizarre level. A quick scan of Laverne was taken to confirm the correct position and the doctor was called in, whom, thank the Lord, was also a woman. I think you can understand why this brought me comfort; being in the position I was in.

"Hello, I'm Dr. Payne," she said.

"Nice to me you. Please excuse me for not getting up," I greeted.

Dr. Payne was careful to explain every step of the procedure. It evidently is a new, state-of-the-art diagnostic tool and aptly so since my breast was also state-of-the-art, at least until they got done with it. She cleansed the area, cold, a pinch (ouch!), as she injects Lidocaine to numb the area. There was the sound of a spring-action trigger as she made a ¼ inch incision in the skin. This would allow her to get the large needle through to the tumor. So far, so good. Another scan had to be taken to make certain the lump had not shifted during the administration of the local anesthetic. The readings were off and Nutmeg rebooted the computer in hopes that it would work correctly. Unfortunately, it did not and she called a repairman. I was still lying on my stomach with Laverne in a chokehold. I feared that it would require the computer to release its vise-grip!

Thank God! There was a manual override and Laverne was released. Thank you, Jesus! Sad to say, Laverne was now hanging 4 inches lower than Shirley and, at my age, I had no illusions that she would snap back! Nutmeg stayed with me offering me comfort and consolation while I held gauze pads over the small incision that had been made in my skin. Dr. Payne was making arrangements to finish the biopsy via ultrasound. I felt sympathy for them both. They had been accommodating and I felt badly about what had happened.

By the time they got me situated on the ultrasound table, it was necessary to give me several more injections to numb the pain. I was introduced to another tech. In keeping with the Spice Girls theme, I'll call her Cinnamon, for the color of her hair. As Cinnamon moved the wand over

Laverne, Dr. Payne was guided to the best areas to inject the anesthetic. This was where she lived up to her name. It's hard to believe that taking tissue samples could be any more painful. Get the picture here. I was surrounded by Cinnamon on Ultrasound, Dr. Payne operating the Tissue Vacuum Gun and Ginger joined us as "the plucker." Cinnamon's wand guided Dr. Payne to the desire area, Dr. Payne would insert the vacuum gun, press a button and tissue from that area would be sucked out into a tiny reservoir where Ginger "plucked" the sample out with tweezers and deposited it into a specimen container. At times, more anesthetic was administered until twelve samples were taken. This entire procedure had to be repeated on Laverne's underside. As pain goes, this was bad. If I ever have to go through it again, I'll insist on something strong to relax me. The mental exhaustion was beginning to take its toll, also.

Butterfly bandages were used to close the incisions. Gauze pads topped with ice packs followed by my bra "rounded out" the most grotesquely shaped breast I'd ever seen. Laverne looked like she had a hangover! When I sat up something didn't feel right in my head. There was a woozy, foggy sensation and my hands were trembling. I asked the doctor what could cause that. She informed me that Epinephrine had been added to the anesthesia to counteract any possible allergic reaction. I told her that I have been treated for Anxiety Disorder for more than twenty years and that the rush of adrenaline (the source of panic attacks) is not a good thing for me. Nutmeg brought me a cup of orange juice to help calm the tremors. I rubbed it on my hands but it didn't help. It was about 1:30 p.m. and I was somewhat sorry to be leaving my new friends. We had a lot of laughs and they'll never know how much they helped me get through it. In fact, after that intimate encounter I suggested they should take Laverne to dinner but Shirley would insist on going, too.

Chapter 4

I'm Not Afraid to Die...Only of Dying Young

When I was a young teen I played a lot of Tennis. I was a natural and spent every waking moment that I was not working or going to school on our neighborhood tennis courts in Southwest Detroit. In the '60's, your hair had to be long and straight and you had to be skinny and have no boobs to be popular. It was not my era. Billie Jean King once said that if your playing with a well-endowed opponent, bring her to the net and make her hit backhand volleys because it was the hardest shot for someone with big boobs. This is not true. Every shot is hard when you have big boobs! One summer my dad decided he wanted me to teach him how to play tennis. This was inadvisable since he had never displayed any athletic ability whatsoever but I would not be pointing that out to him.

We began our first lesson in the handball court where he could get practice making contact between ball and racket. I don't know if men still play handball but just imagine racket ball without the racket. The court my dad and I were in was outdoors, adjacent to the tennis courts. It had a three-sided cinderblock wall and a chain link fence around the rest of the court. The top of those three walls was open but also covered with chain link fencing to prevent the balls from going over to the other side. Our first lesson ended early when Dad decided he could return a ball sailing over his head toward the back fence that was littered with broken glass. I hollered to him to let it go. He didn't listen. I was not surprised. Today his legs bear the tiny scars of sliding onto all that glass.

He decided for his next lesson he would take on playing some of the men his age on the courts. I had been seeing a neighborhood boy named Ron who was into bodybuilding when he decided to show off for some friends. As I walked passed him on the sidelines of the courts, he spontaneously grabbed me and flipped me over his head. I landed on my head and shoulder and literally saw stars. But I remained conscious as I lay on my back looking up into the face of the giggling village idiot who put me there. I thought I was okay until I sat up to go for his throat! That's when my collarbone separated and the meaning of real pain was driven to my brain for the first time.

They called my dad off the court, who was irritated at being interrupted, and he helped me up and supported my elbow and shoulder (since this was the purpose of my now severed collarbone) and proceeded to walk me the dozen or so blocks home. All the while he is scolding me for goofing around and that this was my fault and how much it was inconveniencing him. Dad would frequently call me names and challenge me to go to my room and cry until my eyes swelled. But, I was a stubborn child and refused to give him the satisfaction of knowing I was hurt. Anyway, this lecture continued on the way to the hospital until my mother stepped in and told him it was enough. Throughout this I refused to cry. (Calling Dr. Phil!)

I was sixteen and spent three days in the hospital anticipating surgery. During that stay, a group of interns was brought in to observe the proper way to apply the brace that I would have to wear for the next six weeks. I sat upright in a chair with the instructing doctor standing behind me with the brace. Now, get a mental picture of that. I was naked from the waist up and, even at sixteen, very well endowed. All the boys in junior high called me Chester. Half a dozen young male doctors were lined up directly in front of me to watch. The doctor behind me proceeded to place this brace around the back of my neck, going over my shoulders and back under my arms where he gave a powerful jerk on the straps. which jerks My shoulders shot back and, hence, threw my breasts up into the faces of those doctors! Oh! The humiliation! The embarrassment! I told you that story because it was my first, but not my only, embarrassing moment concerning Laverne and Shirley.

My older sister had breast cancer when she was 42. Hers was non-invasive and detected early during a routine Mammogram. She had a lumpectomy followed by radiation and has been cancer free ever since. That gave me hope. Our mother died when she was 40. I have no idea if she had a genetic predisposition for cancer. About 90% of women diagnosed with breast cancer have no family history of the disease. That's important for women to know. In 2005, 211,240 women and 1,690 men were diagnosed with breast cancer. I was one of those women. I did not know how young 52 was until faced with my own mortality. When my mother died I didn't think 40 was all that young but I was only 21, what did I know? At that time, I couldn't imagine being 52 much less the prospect of facing this dreaded disease. Just for the record, I am not afraid of dying. I am afraid of dying young. My sons are 28 and 32 and I think they still need their mother. I missed out on getting to know my mom as a woman, a friend. My boys and I have become friends and I love that. Of course, mothers think their children can never get along without them no matter how old they are. Just ask one. You may think I'm possessive and controlling, I try not to be but I want to be close by in case they are in want of anything. They'll have children and need me to tell them that Legos *will* pass through the digestive system of a 4-year-old and that when they hear the toilet flush followed by a small voice saying, "Uh-oh," it's already too late.

I have three grandchildren and I don't have to tell those of you who are young grandmothers like me that being a grandma is better than anything else in this world. I want to teach them all the things they need to know that no one else may tell them. For example, if you spray hair spray on dust bunnies and run over them with roller blades, they will ignite. And, no matter how much Jell-O you put in a swimming pool you still cannot walk on water. So many things stroll through your mind when you're waiting to hear news that may seal your fate. And, even though worrying is like shoveling smoke, sometimes it's hard to keep a lock on it. Countless thousands of men and women who have found themselves waiting for results of a biopsy can tell you as many stories. We all don't want to think the worst yet it's lingering overhead like a dark storm cloud.

Chapter 5

No, Virginia, It's Not a Dream...It's a Nightmare

It was Monday morning and the biopsy results were promised to me that day. To their credit, Hooterville Breast Care Center expedited biopsy results for their patients because they realize what their patients are going through during the period of waiting. I had made every effort not to call Dr. B. every hour to see if she received the fax that might change my life. I think I bothered her a couple of times and decided to visit her office on my way home from an errand. It was a long shot but I was getting more anxious by the moment.

They had not received the results yet and it was almost closing time for their office. Nevertheless, they called Hooterville on the chance that they had the results ready. The report was ready so they faxed it over. I was both elated that the wait was over and apprehensive about finally knowing. You see, as long as I didn't know, I was still cancer-free. This can be a dangerous mindset.

A staff member, Candy, escorted me to an exam room. She paused momentarily at the scales and looked at me grinning.

"Oh, no you don't," I warned. "This is a consultation and my weight is irrelevant."

"Girl, I'm just jerking your chain," she laughed. Very funny. Weighing me had become a running joke between us. Before I stepped on the scale, I invariably would remove anything I could to reduce that number, my glasses, bracelets, necklace, shoes, earrings, bridgework and even my gum. She had a special box that she held to receive these items. After ten minutes of preparation I stepped on the scale and weighed 15 pounds more than I had just weighed on my home scale. This happens at every doctor's office. I know their scales are made and purchased by the same outfit that writes those ideal weight charts. It's a cruel conspiracy that I refuse to take part in. I automatically deduct 15 lbs. from their total. I stepped off the scale but, before I was allowed to retrieve my belongings, Candy set the box on the scale to weigh it. It weighed all of 8 ozs. Candy still had that big grin on her face as I put myself back together. I popped my gum back into my mouth and said,

"Hey! 8 ozs. Is 8 ozs."

It didn't take long to convince Candy there was no need for me to strip and put on a paper gown. Now, ordinarily there is little waiting time at Dr. B.'s office but that day seemed an eternity. I had mixed emotions as she came in with her usual greeting.

"Well, hello, Miss Linda. How's my favorite author?" (Okay, I added the favorite author thing.) She stood before me and got right to the point.

"Miss Linda, the density on the underside of your breast is benign. Nevertheless, the tumor on the top of your breast is malignant. It's a grade 3 cancer, aggressive and invasive. You'll need to see a surgeon to remove it followed by Chemotherapy and Radiation Therapy. I can recommend a good surgeon." I don't know how much time elapsed before my reply came.

"That won't be necessary. I know a good surgeon," I said.

Those were the last words I heard. After she left I sat in the room alone for a few minutes replaying every word she said. How is this possible? Not only did I have cancer but it was the most aggressive and invasive form. Chemotherapy? I had always sworn that I would never put myself through that torture. Yet, now I was told that it would be necessary in order to save my life. Wow. That was the first moment it occurred to me that I should have brought my best friend with me, or my sons. I don't think I had expected to need someone with me. The absence of tears at this news sounded a warning blast like a trumpet. If I could not cry at this news, I must really be screwed up.

Always conscious to hide my true emotions, I shrugged on my jacket as I walked down the long hallway to the reception area. You could have heard a pin drop on the carpet. It was then that I realized that Dr. B. had saved me for her last patient to offer me more privacy to grieve. Well, I surprised them all when I reached the front desk. There were four or five staff present with Dr. B. and they all wore solemn expressions.

"You know, I've always told people that I refused to diet because I was storing fat in case I got a terminal disease. I guess the joke's on me!"

There was almost an audible sigh of relief among them. I continued to joke with them and we shared our faith that we knew God is in control even at times like this when we fail to understand His plan for us. Sometime later, when I would feel fear of dying too young, I was reminded that, had God's plan been for this disease to take me out now, He would not have sent a drop of milk to show me in the nick of time. We had all agreed that a positive state of mind would benefit my survival.

Upon arriving home, my best friend, Linda, was taking care of my day care children for me. She asked what the doctor said.

"I have cancer," I whispered so the children would not hear.

"You do not." I guess she had a hard time believing me since I was so emotionally "together."

"Yes, I do. It's aggressive and invasive and I have to call a surgeon as soon as possible. I also have to undergo Chemotherapy and Radiation after surgery."

"I can't believe it," she said.

"Yeah, I know."

I can't remember if we hugged each other. I don't remember her crying which told me how shocked with disbelief she was because she cries at anything. When people talk about feeling nothing I know what they mean. From the moment I got the diagnosis and throughout treatment, this was what I felt more often than not, emptiness, a numbing of emotions. I lost all interest in reading, writing and even socializing with my friends. Any activity that required me to focus was too much effort. Television became my best friend because it asked nothing of me. Friends and the medical community caring for me recommended support groups but I had no desire to talk to anyone about my cancer and what it was already doing to alter my life. I didn't want to talk about it or think about it. A couple of women in my church had started their treatment for breast cancer a few months before I was diagnosed and they expressed feeling much the same way.

I guess it might fall into the category of depression but I was absent of sadness that you usually associate with being depressed. It was like floating through space having no control of what was happening to you. And this was only the beginning of a very long haul.

Chapter 6

Going Under the Knife

My first laugh after the diagnosis came while Linda and I were shopping in Sam's Club. We were in the produce section and I said to her, "I want to get lots of fresh fruits and veggies and start eating healthier." The irony of what I had just said on the heels of being diagnosed with cancer struck me as hilarious. I stopped in my tracks and turned to Linda laughing and said, "Too late!"

Monday morning on May 9, 2005 I was preparing for the Lumpectomy that would be performed by my favorite surgeon, Dr. P. In attendance for this event were my two sons, my daughter-in-law, my best friend, and my dad and stepmother. However, before the operation I was taken to Nuclear Medicine to have a dye injected around the tumor that would travel to the nearest lymph nodes, called the Sentinel Lymph Nodes, and "light them up" so the surgeon knows which ones to remove for biopsy. If the cancer had spread to the lymph nodes these would be the first ones it would reach. This method eliminates the need to remove all the nodes as a precaution.

To say that these injections were painful would be an understatement. One injection I would swear hit the tumor directly! As I did my best to contain the horrific scream that threatened to blow my head off, I focused my pleading eyes on the face of the technician and at that moment I knew I could take him! I vowed then and there that they would

30

never do this to me again without sedation. In fact, that word has become my mantra should further treatment be necessary in the future. Sedation, sedation, sedation!

Back to the party in pre-op, my family was saying their farewells and I asked my dad to say a prayer. Somewhere among the big words he is so fond of he prayed not that God would make the operation a success but that His will would be done even if it meant taking me out! That's right, I kid you not. I thought my youngest son; a Youth Pastor would vault over the gurney and strangle him! But, that's my dad. While I was in surgery, a couple of uncles and cousins drove two hours to take the opportunity to make the event a family reunion in the waiting room. They got so caught up in their revelry, though, that Dad, his brothers and my cousins all took off as soon as they were told that I was not dead. I did not see or hear from Dad for three days and only then because I called him to find out why he could not have waited for me to come out of recovery. I had deluded myself into thinking he drove all the way from Tennessee for me. But, that's my dad. Even as my battle goes on he can't be bothered to pick up a phone to see how I'm doing. But, this isn't about him.

My friends Linda and Miriam stayed with me until they took me to O.R. They got to meet my two newest best friends, the Anesthesiology team. The hospital calls them the Gas-Passers. I told them I was writing a book about my experience and asked them what they wanted to be called. They replied, "Gas X and Gas Y." They explained to me that they would be administering a drug called Versed and went on to tell me how it would make me feel. I said, "I don't care just load me up!"

I managed to make it through the sixties without so much as smoking marijuana. But, if they had introduced me to this drug I would have been hooked! It is as close to Utopia this side of Heaven. It gives you a feeling of floating, no time or space exists and you're in love with everyone you see. I thought that if I did not survive the surgery, what a way to go!

The surgery was a complete success. The tumor, which had grown to 2.5 cm within ten days, was removed with clean margins all around and the Sentinel Lymph Nodes were free from cancer. The report could not have been better. My team of doctors and surgeons knew that time was not on my side with such an aggressive form of cancer.

In recovery, Linda and Miriam came to help me pull myself together enough to get home. Truthfully, I don't remember much about this block of time but they later told very funny stories about trying to get my bra back on. Why they wanted to I have no idea. I would repeat them here but I'm not sure how true they are and this is a non-fiction book. I'm not taking any chances in case I end up on Oprah!

Strange as it may seem, the lump was removed along with an inch all around of clean margin and my breast just morphed back into place. You cannot even tell anything was removed!

Up to now, everything had happened so fast that I still felt a little numb. And I had yet to shed a tear for myself. It was two days later that Linda would be over and I would take my first shower since the surgery. I don't know what prompted it but as I stepped out of the shower and saw myself in the mirror, my body suddenly became racked with sobbing. I bent over the sink and buried my face in the bath towel to muffle my sobs. The anguish I felt was impossible for me to contain. Every Mammogram, every scan, every biopsy, every cut of the scalpel came flooding out at once. I had no idea what prompted the outburst but I was relieved to know that I wasn't an ice princess after all. Linda was soon knocking on the bathroom door and asking if I was all right. Unable to respond to her, she opened the door and came in to see me still burying my face in the towel. She didn't have to ask why I was crying, she knew. That's what's so neat about best friends; you get to know each other so well that sometimes there is no need to explain. She placed her hand on my back to comfort me and said, "Your back is wet."

"Of course it is, you ninny," I blubbered, "I just got out of the shower!" That's when the waterworks stopped and we both had a good laugh.

Chapter 7

God *Is* In Control

When I was about 5 or 6 years old I had necessity to see a dentist for the first time. At the time, Dad was holding a prayer meeting downstairs in our living room and I knew that interrupting would not be welcomed. The pain in my mouth however, had become unbearable and left me no choice. I had been taught since birth that God answers prayer and that he heals people. So how could I get in trouble for believing that? I quietly tiptoed down the stairs. Once in the living room confronted with all those people, I began to second-guess my decision. But, I was there and crying in pain. Of course, everyone gathered around me and prayed for my pain to be gone. Once they were done, Dad dismissed me to go back to bed. I can so clearly remember my thought as I laid my head on the pillow clutching and crying from the still unbearable pain.

"Well, a lot of good *that* did!" I would have the molar extracted the very next day.

I have had questions all my life about why God chooses when and how to heal people. I do believe He heals and I know He could have removed that cancer supernaturally if He had chosen to. But, I have never doubted that His hand was on me and the situation throughout my treatment. It was God who caused that solitary drop of milk to fall directly over the lump so that I would find it in time. And it was the Father who led me, by recommendation, to the finest Oncology team and Surgeons. Their wisdom also came from Him in every decision concerning my treatment. And, by the way, it was God who sent me two angels in the form of businessmen in my church who hired me to open their day care center and gave me the best health insurance they had to offer a full six months before the cancer was diagnosed. I've learned a whole lot more about myself and about Him during the treatment process.

10 Ways You Know That Your Doctor is an Oncologist
by Emily Hollenberg, Cancer Survivor

1. Even though he/she is wearing a white lab coat and not a military uniform, words like battle, fight, war and weapons are frequently used in the conversation.
2. You know that your doctor is an oncologist at a medical center when he/she uses "oma" words like carcinoma, lymphoma and melanoma instead of cancer.
3. He/she tries to explain to you why a low grade is better than a high grade on your path report.
4. He/she wants you to be excited when your tests come back negative not positive, of course this does not fit with most life experiences when you know it is better to be positive than negative.
5. He/she talks a lot about trials and as far as you know is not a lawyer or a judge.

6. When shaking hands with you at your initial appointment, you have a feeling that your veins are being checked out.
7. Asks you if you want a port and you know that this is not an invitation to have a drink.
8. Tells you that you will get a series of treatments and you keep wondering where the "treat" part comes in.
9. Tells you that you are on a protocol and it doesn't seem to fit with the dictionary definition. Protocol: form of ceremony and etiquette observed by diplomats and heads of state.
10. Has you sign a consent form for treatment that is more intimidating than the diagnosis.

My first visit with my Oncologist, Dr. E, was on Monday, May 16th. This would be filled with information about where to go from there. Although the surgery was a success, because the cancer was of the highest grade and most aggressive, Chemotherapy would be next on the agenda. He suggested having Dr. P. insert an infusion port in my chest wall just under the skin to facilitate the chemo more easily. He named off the drug protocol but all I wanted to know was if they could cut it with Versed. I would be scheduled for a total of 8 treatments, spaced twenty-one days apart. Since this is not an instructional manual about cancer treatment, I am going to spare you the technical jargon. Every cancer patient's treatment is designed just for him or her, anyway.

The prognosis for a new cancer occurring was not good so they would be very aggressive in their treatment. Chemotherapy would be followed my 6-8 weeks of daily Radiation Therapy on the affected breast, Laverne. The infusion port was a minor surgery that gave me an opportunity to experience Sedation once again. This port enabled them to access a large blood vessel directly through the port with only a skin puncture.

Before Chemo would begin, I would have to undergo a Bone Scan, Abdominal CT Scan, Chest X-Ray and Mug-a-Scan. These tests would tell the doctor if there were any questionable areas in the rest of my body that needed to be investigated for cancer. My encounter with the scanning machine proved to be uneventful so I see no need to delve into the particulars. Next stop…Chemo.

Chapter 8

An Unforgettable Day

My first Chemo treatment was scheduled for June 2, 2005, and it is a day that I will never forget, but not for the reason you may think. For nearly 30 years I have owned and operated a child day care that I ran in my home. It was an answer to prayer to be able to work from home while raising my two sons as a single parent.

That day, my 2-year-old grandson was in attendance in my day care and, while wrestling with a friend, he broke his leg, his femur to be exact. I suspected it was an injury to his knee and used one of those neck pillows for traveling to immobilize his leg while I waited for my friend to get there to drive us to the hospital. The day care children were left in the care of my assistant while I was gone.

It turned out to be a bad break and he was transported to Children's Hospital to have it set. Fortunately, they did not have to operate to set it. Once they put him to sleep they were able to set the bone and apply a body cast. I was unable to accompany him to the downtown hospital since I had my first Chemo scheduled that afternoon.

My heart was breaking along with his parents and grandparents. We were all a mess of tears and fear and any one of us would have gladly taken his pain for him if we could. I had to leave my precious boy waiting for the transport ambulance.

Rescheduling my appointment was out of the question for me. I understood how important it was to begin Chemo as soon as possible. Being a practical person, I knew that there was no need for me to tag along with my son and daughter-in-law. There was nothing I could do and he was in the best hands possible.

The Chemo would be administered at the clinic of my Oncologist. I was pretty drained of strength by the time I got there and they ask me if I wanted a sedative before beginning. I gazed wide-eyed at my friend and whispered, "Sedation! Yes ma'am, load me up!"

Compared to the events of that day, Chemo was low-key. There were no side effects to experience except the soothing calm that the Ativan offered. I had been told not to expect any reaction until the second or third day after infusion. The port worked like a dream and saved a lot of time and pain chasing down a vein. A little over three hours later, we were on our way home, my first of eight treatments under my belt. Now I just had to wait two days to see how my body would react to the drugs.

I want to tell you here that, the same week I was preparing for the open house of the day care center that I had been hired to start and direct. We had been waiting and preparing for months for the inspection by the licensing consultant scheduled the following week and the open house just two days later. I had been busy enough with my own day care but I also had the licensing process, inspections, buying furniture, supplies and equipment, hiring staff and writing our policies among my tasks. My employers helped tremendously by paying wages for my assistant so I would be free to come and go as needed.

I'm sure that being so busy and having my thoughts preoccupied by business helped me handle the cancer crisis in my life. I know I had a lot of people praying for me and I felt strong. I had more fear of failing my business partners than I did of anything else. This opportunity was a Godsend for me and I wanted so much to be successful. It no longer was just me involved if I fell short. There were thousands of dollars of someone else's money riding on my performance. I admit to you that I felt inadequate for such an undertaking but I believed it's what God wanted me to do.

We were setting up the last two classrooms when the licensing consultant showed up two hours early for her inspection! Thankfully, three hours later, we were granted a license to enroll 140 children and I was elated!

Chapter 9

Hair Today, Gone Tomorrow

The American Cancer Society estimates that a woman in the United States has a 1 in 8 chance of developing invasive breast cancer during her lifetime. About 77% of most breast cancers occur in women ages 50 and older. The good news is that the mortality rate for women of all races combined continues to decline annually.

Two days after my first Chemo I was doubtful that I would survive. I had a horrendous headache that, later, would be found to be the result of a shot of Nuelasta given to me the day after to build white blood cells. Dr. E. had prescribed medication for nausea so what I experienced was minimal. The Chemo seemed to dehydrate me but most of all it weakened me. I would continue to work throughout treatment however I would find it necessary to take off Monday and Tuesday after each treatment because I was too weak to get out of bed. Fortunately, running the day care center was not as physically demanding as it was while in my home. I had competent staff to perform those tasks, now.

Not all Chemo drugs will cause you to lose your hair but I had been assured that I would. Initially, this was not my greatest concern even though I had always taken special care to make a statement with my hair. It was around my third treatment that I began to seriously shed some hair. At the time, I wore my hair in a not-too-short spiked look. During styling, I would spray a section and pull it up with my fingers. Only, now it was just stuck to my fingers, not my scalp. It was really strange because I didn't feel any pulling from my scalp at all. It was as if it had not even been attached in the first place. When I saw that there were too many bald spots to cover, I decided to go for broke and shave it off. Not everyone is comfortable doing this but I didn't want to watch it daily fall away. I opted to wear scarves and caps rather than a wig. Not having hair to worry about was liberating, at first, but it got old, fast, and I began to really miss my hair. I no longer felt attractive because I realized how much my hair contributed to my looks. And, without hair, my head was so small! I would go on to lose my eyebrows, eyelashes and every other hair on my body which all contributed to my feelings of ugliness. I have still not recovered since my hair grew back very curly and smoky gray! During this period I had to admit to being both fat and bald!

Chemo continued to weaken me but my blood count stayed in the normal range throughout the first four treatments, to the amazement of my doctor. However, on the fifth treatment the protocol was changed and a new drug began. If I had gotten off fairly easy up until then, this drug made up for it. Within days of administration, I was dehydrating so rapidly that it was necessary to go back in for IV fluids three times the week following. But, even with that, I was getting increasingly weaker. My white blood count bottomed out and I had to give myself daily injections of Nuepagen that gave me horrible bone pain. I was unable to work all the following week and could barely hold up my head. Just ten days after that fifth treatment I asked Linda to take me to the hospital. I felt like I was dying and I was more scared than I had been so far.

When we got to the ER they took me in immediately and, upon reading my blood pressure, began pushing IV fluids as quickly as they could. The ER doctor was surprised that I was coherent with my blood pressure so low. They had to wait for my pressure to rise in order to administer morphine for my bone pain. I had thrush in my mouth and sores in my nose. It was about twelve hours before they were able to secure a room for me. They were trying to find a private room since I was at risk for infection from low white cell count. It was Labor Day Weekend and the special cancer wing that I needed to be in was closed down. So they had to put me in with the roommate from hell. I won't bore you with details. After all, this is about me, not her.

The fluids did wonders for me and on Monday, Dr. E. came in to see me. I proclaimed to him that I would refuse any further Chemotherapy with this drug. I confess to you that I felt like a coward at that point. I was quitting the treatment that so many before me had endured. Surprisingly, Dr. E. made no attempt to dissuade me. He said that sometimes our bodies simply cannot tolerate certain drugs and that it would do little to help me if it was breaking my system down. He informed me that I had finished the most important drug protocol. That was some consolation to me. I was finished with Chemo and would begin Radiation Therapy as soon as possible. First, I would have Dr. P. remove the infusion port in my chest.

Chapter 10

Nuking Laverne

On September 19th I found myself in the hospital radiology department for the first of many times. In order to receive Radiation Therapy, every inch of Laverne had to be measured as well as calculations made for the permanent settings that would be programmed into the computer controlling the radiation apparatus. In addition, three tattoos would be made, one over my sternum and one on each side of my ribcage. These would be used in lining my body up on the table. I am one of the minority of women I know who has never even wanted to get a tattoo. I have a friend who is also in her fifties who got a smiley face tattoo on her breast when she was in her twenties. To see it now, there is nothing left but a frown! But, now I have three tattooed dots on my torso.

This visit was also necessary so they could make a mold for my head and upper body to lie in during radiation treatments. They called it a cradle. Once they got me positioned just right and all the calculations were made, a large piece of Styrofoam was placed under my head and upper back. They had to make an additional adjustment by slanting the cradle up due to Laverne's tendency to spread out around my throat when I lie on my back. They wanted to avoid radiation to my throat! Finally in place, a warm, thick liquid was poured all around my head, neck and shoulders and I had to remain very still while this molding compound hardened. This cradle would be crucial in assuring that the radiation was administered precisely the same every time.

This entire process took about an hour and a half and was embarrassing to go through. Several personnel, male and female, were in and out and I was totally exposed from the waist up in a very unflattering pose. There would be a total of 35 treatments administered every weekday for seven weeks. I had hoped to take my treatments closer to the center where I worked but during this set-up visit the doctor came in while measurements were being taken. He meekly stood at the side of the table where Laverne lay exposed and politely spoke to me.

"Ms. Coffman, I understand you would like to take your treatments at our Southgate office. There is just one problem with that. Please do not be offended but you have rather large breasts."

"No! They showed you the measurements, didn't they?"

"The problem is that the machine in our Southgate office will not accommodate breast larger than 8 cm. Your breast is 10 cm. so you will need to come to the hospital for your therapy."

"Did you hear that, Laverne? Thanks to you they have to super-size me! Will the humiliation never end?"

Two days later Radiation Therapy began. I sat in the small waiting room in another hospital gown reading framed affirmations hung on the walls to encourage those of us who were unfortunate enough to have reason to be here. I looked around at faces that I would be seeing every weekday for the next two months since most had standing appointments.

Some bore obvious signs of their battle while others looked fairly innocuous. A sudden sadness swept over me, realizing at long last just what I had been facing but not dealing with. It seemed unreal that I should be there and that sadness would mark every single visit to that waiting room for 35 days.

The technicians could not have been friendlier or more accommodating. They led me to the table positioned alongside a huge, round machine waiting overhead. They placed the cradle that had been made at one end and I got on the table and wiggled my head and shoulders into the cradle, my right arm over my head, Laverne exposed again. With techs standing like bookends on each side, they lined up the tattoos with the table and the computer until it was perfect. Leaving the room through a 12" thick metal door, I couldn't help but wonder what future damage might be done in the next two months. In a room across the hall, Laverne and I could be seen on a monitor as the techs began moving the big round monster overhead. Each shot was preceded by a buzzer, four shots on the left and then the monster was moved to Laverne's right side and four more shots were announced.

Someone had a clever idea while designing this room. The ceiling was constructed of Plexiglas light panels with each panel being part of a picture that covered the ceiling, much like pieces of a puzzle. My room depicted what looked like a small harbor town somewhere in New England. By the time my treatments concluded I would know every corner of that picture by heart.

I never got over feeling embarrassed at having to expose my body to so many strangers. I've always been partial to keeping Laverne and Shirley under wraps. The actual treatments were not painful, mostly an inconvenience having them every day. But, as time went on, I began to experience a sunburn effect and special care had to be taken with the newly sensitive skin. Throughout that couple of months I could not wear deodorant or use my usual bath soap. Some people experience more severe damage to their skin but Laverne held up pretty well. She now sports a nice even tan. Shirley is jealous.

One of the aspects of breast cancer treatment that I could not be prepared for was my attitude about my looks. Now, I've never been what you would call beautiful but I was attractive, I think. Once I began treatments, though, I watched all my best physical characteristics gradually trampled under by scalpels, chemo drugs and deadly radiation rays. What remains is a head of hair that lost its natural color and grew back so curly I hate to see my reflection in the mirror, scars on both sides of my neck and breast, 15 additional pounds that found me throughout the inactivity during Chemo, and Laverne and Shirley are no longer twins. I don't know how long it will take me to feel better about my new look, but I sure hope I can get to that point.

I completed Radiation Therapy the first week in December and the techs gave me a certificate and applause. I thought it was a sweet gesture but I left wondering, "Where do I go from here?"

Chapter 11

Strength in Friendship

The year 2005 passed in a blur. I envision a little cartoon car speeding across the T.V. screen with horizontal lines behind to illustrate speed. The car has the number 2005 across its side. From January to November, my life had been consumed with opening a new day care center, running my existing in-home day care in addition to the many facets of breast cancer treatment. By December, I had realized that running the day care center was more pressure than I anticipated and tendered my resignation. That was a harder decision to make than most of the cancer treatment options. My employers had been so good to me and were friends as well. Before I told them of my plans, however, I felt that I should help search for someone to replace me since I knew they would not know what to look for. I located a woman who had just had to close down her center of ten years because she lost the lease on her building. She was a former grade school teacher as well with more than enough experience running her own day care center. The guys were equally impressed and hired her after one interview. It was very difficult for me to admit to myself, as well as to them, that I had done all I could to grow the center and that they needed someone with a following clientele. The new director could provide that. I was a good friend with the mother of one of these businessmen and our relationship suffered for my decision. After all, we mothers are very protective of our children. She and I never really spoke about it, but things are different. I hope she understands, now, that my decision was not a selfish one; I believed that it was best for the organization, too.

The book club that I started three years ago, Sisters Book Club or the Ta-Ta's as we sometimes call ourselves, go on a retreat to northern Michigan every fall. What a time we have, too! All but two of the seven members are members of the "I'm a menopause survivor" club. We have a ritual around the campfire of passing around a Truth Stick and confessing passed misdeeds that are little known to anyone else. There's a little song that we sang one year to the tune of "Do Your Ears Hang Low?" It goes like this.

<u>Do Your Boobs Hang Low?</u>
Do your boobs hang low; do they waggle to and fro?
Can you tie 'em in a knot; can you tie 'em in a bow?
When you throw 'em o'er your shoulders do they hit you like two boulders?
Do your boobs hand low?

Do your under-arms hang, can you waggle them about?
Can you flap 'em up and down as you fly around the town?
Can you semaphore your neighbor with a minimum of labor?
Do your under-arms hang?

Do your buttocks sag making big tracks as they drag?
Do you have to hoist them up as you sit down in the grass?
Does your toilet always flush when you step out of the tub?
Do your buttocks sag?

The Ta-Ta's got me through what cancer brought on. They were continually praying for me, encouraging me and showering me with gifts. Linda, quit her part-time job so she could go with me for my Chemo treatments. They were more than family to me, and still are. We all participated in the Susan B. Komen Race for the Cure in Detroit during the summer of 2006 for the first time and they did it for me. Every woman needs girlfriends like them. Even during my times of self-imposed isolation I always knew that any one of these girlfriends was as close to me as a phone call. That can be such a comfort during the most difficult of times.

It was hard to believe but six months had passed since the original diagnosis and it was time for the first of many regular check-ups in search of any new cancer. Another Mammogram, chest x-ray and CT Scan were ordered by Dr. E. I had perfect peace with this check-up. After all, I had spent the last six months killing off bad and good cells to rid my body of disease. Nothing could have survived the onslaught of Chemo and Radiation. That was the reason I was blindsided by the mass on my liver that showed up on the CT Scan. How was it possible? Knowing that it was on my liver alarmed me. Dr. E. ordered an MRI to get a closer look.

Chapter 12

The MRI

From the morning I found the 1.5 cm lump that would change my life, I had been able to find some humor somewhere, but I had to look. Sometimes, even searching for something to smile about left me empty. But, I have written numerous essays about each step in my dance with cancer. I call it a dance because, as in other areas of my life, I choose to lead. Oh, sure, it's stomped on my toes plenty and dropped me just as I was performing a graceful dip. But, I chose to lead, to be in control as much as possible. On November 19, 2005, my dance with the MRI machine, aka, The Beast, offered a few humorous moments even though it is a dreaded procedure.

The MRI is the subject of many horror stories and I think I heard most of them from the time I announced that I was scheduled for one. The MRI would show the doctors a 3-dimensional view of a mass on my liver that was 2" in diameter. That did not sound good to me and I began to consider the possibility that my life could actually be cut short by this monstrous disease. Dr. E. calmed my fears by telling me that he did not expect it to be malignant since other variables indicating cancer were absent. It did little to calm my fear of having an MRI and neither did well-meaning friends and acquaintances that were all too eager to share the terror of their experience or that of someone they knew.

Normally, I am a little claustrophobic although I had not had an episode in many years. This experience would give new definition to the word.

My doctor suggested that I take one .5 mg Ativan pill just before leaving for the hospital so that I would be calm by the time I started the procedure. If you have ever seen a .5 mg Ativan tablet you know that they are about the size of a freckle. Could only one of these minute pills really calm the fear of this rather robust woman? I took three...on an empty stomach. (Disclaimer: Do not try this at home.)

Linda drove me to the hospital and waited to drive me home since I was sedated. I felt I was capable of driving myself but it makes her feel like she is sharing in my suffering so I try to impose on her whenever I can. I was explaining to her what a piece of cake this was going to be (since I felt absolutely no anxiety), when I stepped out of the car and found the pavement felt spongy. Startled just a little at first, I kept on yakking to Linda as I maneuvered the curb by stepping a foot and a half high only to come down hard on my Reeboks because, of course, the curb was only 4 inches high. Fortunately, Linda's back was to me and she did not see this miscalculation. Like an experienced drunkard, I squared my shoulders and tried to focus more closely on each step. When you're impaired, denial can sometimes save the day. Today was not to be that day.

I thought I was doing rather well until I came to the huge revolving door leading into the lobby of the hospital. Thankfully, Linda went through ahead of me and all I had to do was wait for my opening on the already-revolving door much like I did as a child waiting to jump into a turning jump rope. However, a rope does not have the potential to give you a concussion if you miscalculate and it hits you in the back of the head. Yes. You guessed it! I was a little late on my take off and jumped into the empty space just in time for it to smack me in the back, throwing me face-forward into the front glass. Being a very agile person I managed to stay on my feet, at least until the door spit me out into the lobby where the jig was up! Linda turned to find me crawling on all fours to the nearest chair so I could pull myself up off the floor. Her jaw dropped but, before she could express her surprise, I beat her to the punch with an attempt at lightness.

"Pushed that door a little fast, didn't ya?" I accused.

"Oh, my gosh! I am so sorry, Honey! Are you alright?"

"I'm fine, I'm fine. Just slow down a little."
Folks, you can sometimes find a way to preserve your dignity by turning the tables on a friend who is only too willing to take the blame!

Linda took a seat while I signed in on the dotted line…well, one of the dotted lines. As we sat waiting to be called in, we were catching up on events of the previous week when she asked me a question and got no response. Repeating herself, I managed a coherent answer but I have no recollection of the question or the answer. Skipping to the chase, so to speak, the tech came to get me and I slowly followed him to a trailer where I was to receive my MRI scan. The trailer that housed The Beast did nothing to boost my confidence but I didn't care at that point. I was asked to remove my glasses, the cap that kept my baldhead concealed and my bra.

"Okay by me," I said, "but you really should buy me dinner first."
Entering the room where The Beast stood sentry consumed almost every square inch of space. The table that I was told

to lie on looked to be no more than 12 inches wide. Where was the table for the other half of me? Peering into the long tube-like opening, "the mouth of The Beast," where I would be entombed for close to an hour, I had just one question for the technician.

"Is that opening adjustable? Because, if it isn't there is no way you are going to fit me in there!"

"Oh, sure we will. You'll be surprised. We'll make you fit."

Now I wanted to ask this kid if he thought I was made from Play-Doh but I suddenly was not sure of my name. So, like a Lemming, I followed his directions to lie down on the 12-inch wide table while holding tightly to a tech on each side.

"Are you on it?' one asked me. "Can you let go, now?"

"Sure, why not?" I mumbled. At the moment of release, my arms fell past my sides plummeting toward the floor like a faulty parachute!

"Whoa!" my cowboys exclaimed as they took control again.

"Where do I put my arms?' I inquired.

"Try putting them above your head."

That was simple enough and might have worked had Laverne and Shirley not fallen to each side and nearly bounced off the floor!

"I don't see that working," I chuckled.

"Well, hold them against your sides until we get you in there."

He gave me earplugs, which I promptly stuck into my ears until I saw his lips moving and took them back out.

"Are you saying something to me?"

54

"I was saying that I will be talking you through this all the way."

"How is that going to happen if I'm wearing earplugs?"

"I'll talk loud," he assured me.

Thank heavens I have a technician with a scientific mind! A foam rubber window-pane-like piece was placed on top of my stomach and I was informed that it was an antenna.

"Can I get cable in there?" For a moment I saw a ray of hope.

Over the antenna they placed a sheet to keep down the friction, and, in my case friction would be an action verb throughout this procedure, while the table was moving me into the tomb, which can best be described as trying to squeeze toothpaste back into the tube! I now knew where they expected my arms to rest. They were squeezed tightly against my sides, pushing my breasts to the forefront of my chest that was now pressing the antenna against the ceiling of The Beast. I could have pulled in radio-free Europe but would have settled for HBO. As I was being squeezed deeper into the abyss, I could hear a sound similar to fingernails on a chalkboard and realized that this is the sound the friction makes when bare flesh comes in close contact with fiberglass and steel. But, I had to hand it to them; they got me to fit, barely. They had put a rubber bulb in my left hand that, I was told; a gentle squeeze would summon them if I needed help. Only minutes later I would realize that it was not possible because both my hands had gone numb from lack of circulation. Later, I would discover that the bulb was connected to **nothing**! Talk about your placebo!

The sounds from the tomb can best be described as someone drumming their fingers on the top followed by intermittent loud buzzing and the sound of a washing machine agitating. Friends had told of the awful noise and the closed-feeling. I had no time to be concerned with anything but trying to get blood to my fingers. Halfway through the process I was brought out once to receive an injection of some substance that would help with contrast in the films. I forewarned them that my blood vessels were small, deep and had a tendency to roll. After three sticks they informed me that they were not rolling, they were running! Not to be outdone, they finally tapped into one and the injection was accomplished. As the female tech injected the substance, she asked the "kid" to start the machine. The table began moving me back into the tomb as she was hollering for him to hit the stop button. However, The Beast had a mind of it's own and, just when they thought they had it stopped, it began pulling me farther into it's mouth. Needle still in my vein, she was dancing backwards to keep up with the runaway table, trying to inject the drug before I disappeared into oblivion. Finally extricating the needle from my arm, I was ready for a few more close-ups.

As it turned out, it was not the horror that had been depicted to me. I told the technicians that I was a writer and thanked them for giving me some great material. I promised them I would change their names to protect their bumbling. By now, the Ativan had worn off somewhat as I was led back to the waiting room to retrieve my driver.

"So, how was it?" Linda asked.

"Piece o' cake," I replied.

Chapter 13

Bosom Buddies

There is something extraordinary that occurs among cancer patients for which I was not prepared. Being a rather solitary person, I run my businesses in my home and, except for running errands and going to church, I do not often socialize, and when I do it's with long-time friends. However, I found that there appears to be an unspoken bond among those battling cancer. Throughout Chemo and Radiation I did not get to know anyone on a personal level, not even enough to learn their names. Yet, while Chemo was being administered or while in the waiting room for Radiation Therapy, histories were shared as if we all needed to tell someone what we were going through. Surprisingly, attitudes, without exception, were positive. One particular instance that stands out in my mind was when I had to attend the Chemo clinic on an unscheduled day to have fluids infused because the new drug they had started me on was rapidly dehydrating me, I was dragging and weak and fighting back tears. I was feeling that all it would take for me to die would be for me to lie down and just give up the ghost. An older woman wearing a print scarf to warm her hairless head was hooked up to her "lifeline" of drugs. As I shuffled past her she looked at me with sympathetic eyes and said to me, "Oh, Honey, I'm sorry you're having a bad day. It'll get better." That was when I lost my battle to keep my tears contained.

The only time I have ever been disappointed in Dr. E. was on that particular day. I chalk it up to his being a man. I was sobbing uncontrollably so the nurse sent for Dr. E. while she accessed my infusion port to administer the fluids. Dr. E. entered the small private room and asked me what was wrong. Ha! "I have breast cancer and that new drug you gave me is going to beat the disease in killing me!" What I really said was, "Boo hoo, sob, sob." My brilliant oncologist didn't miss a beat and stated, "I think you are depressed." Throughout the ages, men have never been able to handle a crying woman. He wrote me a script for a sedative, which I discarded when I got home, since I was already on Zoloft and Ativan to treat the Panic Disorder that I had battled for the last 25 years. The nurse injected Ativan into my IV and in a few seconds, to Dr. E.'s relief, the waterworks stopped. Linda was with me that day, too, feeling helpless. I would have to go in for more fluids two more days that same week and by the weekend Linda would have to take me to the hospital emergency room. I was reminded of a joke I had recently read.

"Why did the chemo patient cross the road?"

"She was hoping to get hit by a truck!"

One thing I learned about myself during treatment was that I am much stronger than I ever thought. B.C. (before cancer), if you had told me that I would consent to undergo Chemotherapy I would have said, "Never!" And, to this day, I confess that I did not consent so much for myself as for my sons and my grandchildren. You see, as I said before, I think they still need me and I am determined to be there on the sidelines ready to go in at a moment's notice.

My sons were my motivation for beating the Panic Disorder, also. More than thirty years ago I lost my mother. She was only 40, I was 21 and had just given birth to my first son. That is what, I am told, triggered the panic attacks. It was several years before more was known about the disorder and the appropriate drugs administered to help deal with the horrifying symptoms. By then, I was raising my boys as a single parent and they were my sole reason for not giving up. I hired people to help me run the day care since I could not be alone due to the extreme anxiety and drugs I had to take to deal with it. It took many, many years and God carrying me much of the time, but today I feel victorious. Many people are confined to their homes due to the Agoraphobia that ensues. But, I could not let my boys down. The doctor treating my anxiety recently asked me, "This cancer….it's the worst thing you've gone through in your life?" I replied, "No, the panic disorder holds that distinction." You see, all of my life in the difficult times, I have always compared them with the panic disorder and I found strength in knowing that I had already been through the worst. The breast cancer holds a solid second place and I am not done fighting, yet. But, I won't quit because my sons may need me to pinch hit for them and I want to be found in the batter's box.

Cancer...It Won't Get The Breast of Me

Chapter 14

I've Always Liked Liver

I know you're waiting with baited breath to know the results of the MRI. What could have been a less than ideal result turned out to be two cysts, two harmless cysts. What a relief! I felt like I had a new lease on life. Just a couple more radiation treatments and I would be done. My six-month CT scans showed my body to be free of cancer. I was not surprised since, I doubt, any cancer cell could have survived the onslaught of Chemo and Radiation. Thanksgiving would be especially sweet that year with my sons and me giving God thanks for my recovery.

It would be several months before I grew enough hair to ditch my scarves and hats but Laverne was relieved that she could now heal from the extreme sunburn. I had given my notice and recommended my replacement at the day care center had been hired. The New Year, 2006, would be a new start for me. I reopened my home day care and was looking forward to six months of being left alone by the medical community.

My January checkup with Dr. E. brought good news and a surprise. The good news was that my treatment had been successful and there was no longer evidence of cancer. I was cautioned, however, of the likelihood that a new

60

cancer might occur. He recommended a yearlong regimen of Herceptin infusions, one infusion every week for fifty-two weeks. This new "smart" chemo drug would attack any cancer cells while leaving my good cells alone. There were few known side effects with one exception, heart failure. Heart failure!

"Do I get any forewarning if it is effecting my heart?" I asked.

"Of course. If the drug is affecting your heart you will experience shortness of breath and fatigue," he replied.

"That's not a great help, Doc, since I am always tired and short of breath! Give me a little more to go on, here."

"We will perform a Muga-Scan on your heart before we begin and repeat it every three months to keep a check on your heart. I suggest you have your surgeon put the infusion port back in because it's going to be a long haul."

Now, you must understand that I went into this meeting with my Oncologist believing it to be a mere formality. The last thing I expected was more Chemotherapy. I am glad that he is being aggressive with my treatment since the cancer is very aggressive and invasive. He also agreed with my "groinocologist," Dr. B. that it would be a good idea to undergo an Oopherectomy.

"Excuse me? Just where are my Oophers and why do they have to come out?" I asked.

"That is the term used when your ovaries are removed. Since Ovarian Cancer is very hard to detect early, it is best if you have them removed. At your age they're shrunken and shriveled up, anyway. You don't need them. I also am writing you a prescription for a new Chemo drug called Femara. You must take one tablet each day for the next five years to help retard the onset of cancer in your breast again. Do you have any questions?"

Oh, I had questions, none of which came to mind. My "routine" checkup had become a nightmare. I would be "living" with cancer even while in remission. It would be hard to think of myself as a survivor as long as the threat existed. I had come through so much and yet I was not finished. For the first time since the cancer proclamation by Dr. B. I felt heavy with dread and sadness.

Top Ten Ways To Know You Are A Cancer Survivor

10 Your alarm clock goes off at 6 a.m. and you're glad to hear it.

9. Your mother-in-law invites you to lunch and you just say NO.

8. You're back in the family rotation to take out the garbage.

7. When you no longer have an urge to choke the person who says, "all you need to beat cancer is the right attitude."

6. When your dental floss runs out and you buy 1000 yards.

5. When you use your toothbrush to brush your teeth and not comb your hair.

4. You have a chance to buy additional life insurance but you buy a new convertible car instead.

3. Your doctor tells you to lose weight and do something about your cholesterol and you actually listen.

2. When your biggest annual celebration is again your birthday, and not the day you were diagnosed.

1. When you use your Visa card more than your hospital parking pass.

Chapter 15

Tag-Team Recovery

There is a story told about a man who was not feeling well so his wife dragged him to the doctor. After running a battery of tests, the doctor asks to speak privately to his wife. He tells her that her husband has cancer. The wife asks, "Can he be cured?" The doctor replies "there's a chance we can cure him with chemotherapy, but you will need to take care of him every day for the next year…cooking special meals, cleaning up the vomit, changing the bed pan, driving him to the hospital for daily treatments, and so on." When the wife comes out to the waiting room, the husband asks her what the doctor said, his wife answers, "He said that you're going to die."

I opened this chapter with that story because I want to talk about support systems for the cancer patient. No matter how brave you think you are or want to be, you will need people to help you get through what this disease brings to interrupt your life. It includes those who transport or accompany you to treatments, provide you with meals, do your shopping and cleaning, pray for you, call you and send cards or just hold a cold wash cloth to your head. This is your support system and they are indispensable to you!

Throughout my treatments I wanted to retreat into my private cocoon. I live with my oldest son so I was not alone which greatly helped. I looked forward to the daily delivery of mail because it never failed to bring cards from well-wishers, some of whom were mere acquaintances. The telephone calls were few. I think most people had no idea what to say to me or how I might be feeling. Most would ask Linda how I was doing and she would encourage them to call me. My pastor was a great source of prayer and encouragement for me. He would show up at the hospital even when I told him it was not necessary. The day care center was located in our church so he came to me on a daily basis to ask if there was anything I needed. My employers, the owners of the center, frequently inquired about my health and reminded me to take care of my health needs above all else. They were also paying for the best health insurance money can buy as well as affording me paid time off whenever I needed it. These men are truly godly men and He blesses their business endeavors because of it. Linda had quit her part-time job to go with me to Chemo, surgeries and whatever else I needed. Two of my sisters regularly sent me care packages. My older sister crocheted bags, rags, hats, shawls and anything else she could imagine that could be woven from yarn. My younger sister sent books, DVDs, and hair care products in anticipation of my hair growing back some day. They were among the few that I felt like talking to on the phone. They live out of state.

To fellow Christians I would like to add that you might find it difficult to pray for yourself. I know I did. It wasn't that I was mad at God or any such thing; I just did not know what to say. This is one of the times when being a part of a local church body really works for you. People in my church family would approach me, on the Sunday mornings that I was able to attend service, and tell me that God kept bringing my name to their mind to pray for me. Some of these people I only knew by face, yet, they were praying for me. People I had not been in touch with for some time sent cards and gifts. If I had not been sure that I was not dying this might have alarmed me. But, just the thought of cancer strikes fear in the hearts of everyone. I never considered that I would have cancer since there was no family history until my older sister was diagnosed with breast cancer. Still, when I received my diagnosis, it was hard to believe. My church family was also part of my support system and they may not realize how much their prayers did for me.

Not the least of them, my sons Jason and Adam and my daughter-in-law, Laura, were constant support. They prayed for me. Even my now 3-year-old grandson prayed for his Nana. I know little of what was going through my sons' minds since men seem to internalize their feelings. Laura would frequently call me and inquire about a test or procedure or to find out what the latest doctor had to say. I should mention here, also, that Laura's mother, Margaret, who I count as a good friend, was a great help in recommending the many specialists I needed. She had battled cancer twice already and, having worked at the hospital I would frequent, knew the best of the best. Jason took over as cook, housekeeper, shopper, etc. during that long year. It was so comforting just having him near me. Adam is a youth pastor and he enlisted his group in praying for me. I think it was especially hard on him because he had recently lost a very good friend, only 19 years old, to cancer. He spent a lot of time with him and his family until he lost his battle. Shortly after, the wife of another friend and mother of two small children lost her battle with cancer. His strength amazes me.

B.C. (before cancer) I had considered myself somewhat of a loner. I had no idea how many people really cared about me. I wish I could say that I have been as good a friend to them but I doubt it. If you're having your own dance with cancer, you may be surprised at the support team surrounding you. Most will not know what you need at a particular time but will be glad to hear you tell them. There are many online groups and websites that can offer support. My hospital cancer center was a wealth of information about services for cancer patients. The important thing to remember is that you don't have to go through this alone. Help is there, just ask.

Chapter 16

Living with Cancer

To date, I am cancer-free but not free of cancer. I am learning to live with the reality that this disease may rear its ugly head again at any time. I will continue getting weekly Herceptin infusions until January, 2007 in hopes that it will keep the cancer at bay a little longer. I experienced my first Colonoscopy this week, the first of many in my future. I couldn't help but ask my colorectal surgeon what prompted him to enter this particular field of medicine.

"I like to play golf," he said.

"Is that what you had in mind, 18 holes a day?" I quipped.

The only inviting aspect of my Colonoscopy was...you guessed it...sedation. Sedation enabled me to see the humor in the experience. For instance, I now know how a Muppet feels. During the procedure so many questions came to mind, such as:

- "Find Jimmy Hoffa, yet?"
- "Can you hear me NOW?"
- "Are we there yet?"
- "You know, in Arkansas, we're now legally married."
- "Any sign of the trapped miners, Chief?"

- "You put your left hand in, you take your left hand out...you do the Hokey Pokey..."
- "Hey, Doc, let me know if you find my dignity."
- "Does your mother know what you do for a living?"
- "I have a name for my colon now...the Outback Snakehouse!"

The test results were excellent, clean as a whistle. I'm glad that's *behind* me for another year!

It's been three months since I have seen my Oncologist. I am scheduled to visit Dr. E. next month and we will begin scans again, ever in search of cancer's return. Although these scans are an inconvenience, they are painless and afford me the peace of mind that comes with knowing that this disease will not sneak up on me. And that is the key to its cure, early detection. Even though some procedures are uncomfortable, such as the Mammogram and Colonoscopy, I highly recommend that you undergo the discomfort for the sake of being informed. Denial has never cured a disease and, in fact, has helped to populate our cemeteries with people who left us before their time. ***Not knowing is not better, it can be dangerous.*** I don't know if my future will include another cancer but I will not let it catch me unaware. And I will not let it define who I am. Great discoveries in cancer research are being made every day and every year more and more women are living as breast cancer survivors. If, someday, I lose my battle with cancer it will not be because I refused testing or treatment, it will be because it was my time to go.

I have learned valuable lessons throughout the last year. For one, I learned that I am a lot stronger than I thought. Secondly, every day offers me 24 more hours to enjoy my family, friends, nature and making a difference in the lives of the children in my care. I can take advantage of it or squander it; it's up to me. But, tomorrow is not promised to any of us. Thirdly, I will obsess less about things that I detest such as dieting and exercise. I am willing to bet that most the women on the Titanic turned down dessert after their last meal! Finally, I will not feel guilty about enjoying my leisure time and indulging in my passion for reading and writing fiction. I want no regrets from here on out.

So, if you are going through a battle with cancer, or any disease for that matter, once you get over the shock and grief, take control. You may not see what you could possibly learn from your tragedy but sometimes you have to look for it. And most of all, find opportunities to laugh. Laughter really does the body good, like medicine, as the Bible tells us. I hope reading about my experience has brought some laughter to you.

Other books by L.S. Coffman

About the Author

This book is L. S. Coffman's first work of nonfiction chronicling her treatment for Breast Cancer. She has also published a novel, "Sentenced To Redemption" and two children's picture books. She is most proud of her two grown sons and her three grandchildren. She resides in a suburb of Detroit, MI.

For more info and to purchase her books online visit:
www.lscoffman.com

2896219

Made in the USA